A lot of our food comes from **plants**.

Some foods can be eaten just as they grow—naturally.

Food can be changed by cutting, heating, cooling, or combining with different food items.

We use natural resources to make things we need or want. We can combine different natural resources or change them to meet our needs.

All of these things are made by people. They are man-made.

Everything around us either comes from nature or is man-made.

The things that come from the Earth are called natural resources. These are all things that can exist without humans' help. Plants, animals, sunlight, air, water, soil, oil, natural gas, rocks, and minerals are natural resources.

Natural or Man-made?

A Compare and Contrast Book

Trees are plants. We use trees to make things we need in many different ways.

We use lumber from pine trees to build houses.

Lumber from other types of trees (like cherry, oak, or mahogany) may be used to make furniture or some of the toys you play with.

We eat nuts and fruits that grow naturally on trees.

Maple and rubber trees are tapped so that the sap drips into buckets. We use the sap to make maple syrup and rubber.

Even paper and pencils come from trees!

We use both plants and **animals** to make clothing!

Cotton cloth is made from the cotton plant. You might even be wearing a cotton t-shirt right now.

The wool we use to make sweaters, gloves, hats, and blankets usually comes from sheep fur. We might also use fur from goats, llamas, or even rabbits.

We make leather from cows and other animal skins. We use leather for shoes, belts, gloves, and coats.

The meat we eat comes from a variety of different animals. Many animals are raised on farms for their meat. Other animals are caught or hunted in the wild.

We cut and cook most of our meat to eat.

We can even use **sunlight** and **air** to support our needs. We convert energy from the sun (solar) and moving air (wind) into electricity.

We might not be able to hold air (a form of matter) in our hands, but we can make it fit our needs. We use it to keep tires and balls full.

Sometimes we use **water** in its natural state, but we move it or contain it to meet our needs.

Like many other animals, humans need to drink water to survive. We might drink water out of plastic bottles or straight from the tap.

Plants need water too. Rain waters plants. We sometimes water gardens and farm fields.

We swim in water to stay cool in hot weather.

We use water to clean things— including ourselves!

We use water to cook.

We convert energy from moving water into electricity.

There are many kinds of **soils** in different habitats. You can see differences in color and texture of soils. The texture of soil determines how much water it can hold. Different types of plants need different types of soils. We plant crops in the soil they need.

Rocks and **minerals** are natural resources that may take thousands of years to form. There are many different kinds that we cut or use to meet our needs:

- Marble is cut and shaped to make statues.
- Granite is often cut and used for kitchen countertops.
- Slate is cut and used for roof shingles or garden-path rocks.

Sand is mixed with chemicals to soften it and then melted to make glass.

Concrete is a mixture of sand, rocks, and water that is shaped and then dried.

We even use minerals, like diamonds, to make jewelry.

Aluminum is used to make soda cans and foil.

Oil and natural gas are natural resources found deep underground. We get them by drilling down and pumping them to the surface.

The gas used in your car comes from the oil in the ground. We also use oil to make plastic for toys, drink bottles, and food wraps. Even the crayons you use to color use oil in them!

Many people use natural gas to heat their homes and to cook on a stove or a grill.

What natural resources do you think were used to make these changed or man-made items?

How might you use these natural resources?

For Creative Minds

Simple Changes to Food

Sometimes changing natural resources to fit our needs is as simple as washing and cutting, chopping, or blending. After we have changed the shape, we might use as is, cook, or freeze. Can you identify how we use these natural resources?

hard-boiled eggs

tomato slices

strawberry popsicle

grapes

cucumbers

fish

As is: tomato slices (sliced), cucumbers (sliced), grapes (can also be frozen)

Cooking: hard-boiled egg (cooked, peeled & cut), fish (cut and cooked)

Freezing: strawberry popsicle (blended and frozen), grapes (cleaned and frozen)

Match the Natural Resource to the Food

1

corn

Sometimes it's easy to tell what things are made from which natural resources. Other times, there have been so many changes made that it's hard to tell.

We eat corn on the cob and popcorn. What are some other foods made from corn?

A

ice cream

2

wheat

We eat a lot of food made from flour ground from wheat. Almost any cereal or cracker has wheat in it. What are some other things made with wheat?

B

tortilla chips

3

cow

Cows give us meat (beef) and clothing (leather). Most of the dairy we eat and drink also comes from cows. In addition to milk, butter, and cheese, what other dairy products do we eat?

C
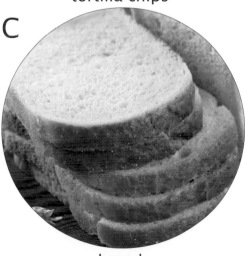
bread

Answer: 1 corn: B tortilla chips; 2 wheat: C bread; 3 cow: A. ice cream

What Came From Rocks and Minerals?

concrete sidewalk

diamond ring

apples

building

cotton cloth

kitchen counter

aluminum cans

stone bridge

glass

Answer: everything except the apples and cotton cloth

What Came From Trees?

maple syrup

pencils

wooden puzzle

house frame

rubber bands

walnuts

oranges

toy train tracks

books (paper)

Answer: everything

Thanks to Chip Lindsey, Senior Director of Education at the Children's Museum of Pittsburgh, for verifying the accuracy of the information in this book.

All photographs are licensed through Adobe Stock Photos or Shutterstock.

Library of Congress Cataloging-in-Publication Data

Title: Natural or man-made? : a compare and contrast book.
Description: Mt. Pleasant, SC : Arbordale Publishing, LLC, [2021] | Series: Compare and contrast book | Includes bibliographical references.
Identifiers: LCCN 2021013701 (print) | LCCN 2021013702 (ebook) | ISBN 9781643518244 (paperback) | ISBN 9781643518381 (adobe pdf) | ISBN 9781643518527 (epub) | ISBN 9781643518664
Subjects: LCSH: Natural resources--Juvenile literature. | Manufactures--Juvenile literature.
Classification: LCC HC85 .N3526 2021 (print) | LCC HC85 (ebook) | DDC 333.7--dc23
LC record available at https://lccn.loc.gov/2021013701
LC ebook record available at https://lccn.loc.gov/2021013702

Bibliography
"Aluminum | Minerals Education Coalition." Minerals Education Coalition, 2016, mineralseducationcoalition.org/minerals-database/aluminum/.
Chisholm, Kirk. "144 Products Made from Petroleum and Some That May Shock You." Innovative Advisory Group, 27 Jan. 2015, www.innovativewealth.com/inflation-monitor/what-products-made-from-petroleum-outside-of-gasoline/.
Common Types of Stones Used in Construction. 17 Apr. 2016, constructionheadline.com /type-stone-construction.
Oil and Natural Gas Reserves: Availability, Extraction and Use Video. "Oil and Natural Gas Reserves: Availability, Extraction and Use - Environment & Ecology Class (Video) | Study.com." Study.com, 2021, study.com/academy/lesson/oil-and-natural-gas-reserves-availability-extraction-and-use.html#transcriptHeader. .
"What Are 4 Types of Soil?" Garden Guides, www.gardenguides.com/94506-4-types-soil.html.

Lexile Level: 760L

Printed in the US
This product conforms to CPSIA 2008
First Printing

Arbordale Publishing, LLC
Mt. Pleasant, SC 29464
www.ArbordalePublishing.com